Jane
Inouye

DANIEL INOUYE

DANIEL INOUYE

by Jane Goodsell

illustrated by Haru Wells

Thomas Y. Crowell Company · New York

CROWELL BIOGRAPHIES · *Edited by Susan Bartlett Weber*

Library of Congress Cataloging in Publication Data. Goodsell, Jane. Daniel Inouye. SUMMARY: A biography of the first Congressman from the state of Hawaii who was also the first American of Japanese descent to serve in the Congress of the United States. 1. Inouye, Daniel K., 1924-   —Juv. lit. 2. Legislators—United States—Biography—Juv. lit. [1. Inouye, Daniel K., 1924-   2. Legislators] I. Wells, Haru. E840.8.I5G66   328.73'092'4   [B]   77-1405   ISBN 0-690-01358-2 (lib. bdg.)

2 3 4 5 6 7 8 10

DANIEL INOUYE

A CROWELL BIOGRAPHY

It was his first day on the job yet everyone knew who he was. Visitors pointed him out from the balcony that overlooked the huge room with its many rows of seats. "He's the new Congressman from Hawaii," they whispered.

It was easy to spot the short, brown-faced man with the quick smile. He was the first American of Japanese descent ever to serve in the Congress of the United States. People recognized him, too, by his empty right sleeve, tucked neatly into his pocket. They remembered that he had lost an arm in the war.

His name was Daniel Ken Inouye (In-NO-way) and he felt excited and proud to be where he was, seated in the House of Representatives in Washington, D.C. But he was a little scared, too. Here in this room he would help to make the laws of his country. He was the first Congressman ever elected by the brand new state of Hawaii. Daniel Inouye knew that he had a big job ahead of him, and he had a lot to learn. Yet he felt sure that he would be a good Congressman if he worked hard and did what he felt was right. It helped, as it often did, to remember something his mother had said to him many years before.

"Mama," he asked one day, "could a poor boy like me grow up to marry the daughter of the Emperor of Japan?"

Dan's mother answered him seriously. "Never forget," she said, "that you are as good as anyone else. But remember, too, that you are no better than anyone else either."

Dan's mother knew that it was important for him to believe this. In Hawaii, where the Inouyes lived, people who had brown skin were looked down on by whites.

Dan's family was Japanese-American, and he and his brothers and sister were *nisei*. This is a term for children of Japanese descent born in America to parents who have moved there from Japan. Both Japanese and American customs were kept in the Inouye house. The family used chopsticks to eat Japanese food, and knives and forks to eat American food.

Dan, who was born in 1924, was the oldest child. He was expected in the Japanese way to look out for the younger children in the family. Dan spoke Japanese before he learned English. He went to an American school, but he spent two hours every afternoon at a Japanese school. He was sent there to learn the history and customs of the country of his ancestors. But the Inouyes did not think of Japan as their country. They were citizens of the United States, and they pledged allegiance to the American flag.

This is true of everyone born in Hawaii today. But it was not always so.

Hawaii is made up of a long string of islands near the middle of the Pacific Ocean about 2,100 miles from San Francisco. The first people to make the islands their home were called Polynesians. They sailed there in canoes over two thousand years ago. Nobody knows exactly when, or where they came from.

These tall, handsome, brown-skinned people lived peacefully for many years on the beautiful islands which were unknown to the rest of the world. The Polynesians were ruled by kings and queens, and they worshipped many gods.

Then one day in 1778 two great sailing ships with tall masts came into view. Aboard one of the ships was the English explorer James Cook. Captain Cook's discovery of the islands brought many changes. News spread of the lovely green valleys, warm sunshine and tall palm trees, and other ships sailed there to drop anchor in the dark blue water.

The first Americans to settle in Hawaii were missionaries. They came in 1820, over 150 years ago, to persuade the Polynesians to give up their gods and become Christians. The missionaries learned that sugar cane grows well in the rocky soil and warm climate of Hawaii. They planted

it in big fields which were called plantations. Other Americans heard of the money that could be made growing sugar cane, and they came to Hawaii to start plantations, too. Large numbers of workers were needed to plant and harvest the cane. The planters hired people from other countries who were willing to work for very low pay.

Some, like Dan's grandparents, came from Japan. Others came from China, Portugal, Korea and the Philippine islands. They lived on the plantations in small, ugly shacks and sometimes worked fifteen hours a day in the fields. For this, they earned only a few dollars a month.

The plantations produced a great deal of cane which was made into sugar. Thousands of tons of sugar were shipped each year to the United States. The families that owned plantations and sugar companies became rich. But they worried that the American government might pass laws which would make it harder to sell so much sugar to the United States. Some Americans felt that it hurt the United States to spend so much money outside the country.

Businessmen in Hawaii got together and figured out a way to keep such laws from being passed. Hawaii could become a part of the United States. Then Americans could no longer say that money paid to Hawaii went out of their own country.

The businessmen convinced many people that their idea was a good one. They did not do it by saying that it would make more money for the sugar industry. Instead they argued that the United States could govern Hawaii better than the Hawaiians themselves could under their kings and queens.

Not everyone in the American government wanted Hawaii to join their country. Some were against it because they felt that the islands should be governed by the Hawaiians who were there first. This was a fair reason. But others believed that only people with white skin should be American citizens, and half the people in Hawaii were Asians whose skin was brown.

The people in the islands who wanted to join the United States were determined not to give up. In 1893, they forced the queen who then ruled to give up her throne, and they took over the government themselves. Five years later, they got what they wanted. The United States Congress voted to make Hawaii an American territory.

A territory does not have the rights and powers of a state. People in Hawaii could elect a delegate to send to the United States Congress, but the delegate could not vote. They could form political parties, and elect Democratic and Republican representatives to a territorial legislature. But the legislature had little power. The islands were ruled by a governor who was appointed by the President in Washington, D.C.

Still, Hawaii was now American. All islanders who could read and write—white and brown-skinned people of many races from many lands—became American citizens.

Like the Inouyes, most Japanese-American families sent their children to American schools where they spoke English and played American games. The children thought of George Washington and Abraham Lincoln as men who had been presidents of their own country. They meant every word when they pledged allegiance to the American flag.

The Inouyes were poor, but this did not bother Dan when he was growing up. His house in a crowded slum was small and cramped, but his friends lived in houses like that, too. And though he often left the table feeling a little hungry, that was easy to fix. He could fill up on the delicious fruits that grow wild in Hawaii. It did not bother Dan

either that his shoes were bought two sizes too big, and had to be stuffed with paper until he grew into them. He didn't like to wear shoes anyway. In warm, sunny Hawaii it was much nicer to go barefoot.

All year round Dan speared fish and rode surfboards to shore on long curling ocean waves. He had many hobbies. He collected stamps and raised homing pigeons and tropical fish. He played the piano and the saxophone. To earn money, he worked as a baby-sitter and mowed lawns and cut his friends' hair. He liked best the job of beach boy.

He was paid by the tourists who stayed at the big hotels to paddle their surfboards out to where the big waves broke. Dan showed them how to balance standing up on the boards. Then he shoved them off to ride the breakers to shore.

Yet in some ways Hawaii was not an easy place to grow up. Whites, or *haoles* as they are called in the islands, did not want their children to be friends with brown-skinned boys and girls who spoke what seemed to them an odd language.

Many Asian families in Hawaii spoke another language before they spoke English. It is not easy to learn a second language, especially when one's friends have a hard time speaking it, too. So people spoke English mixed with Japanese, Chinese, and Hawaiian words. Often they did not follow the rules of English grammar. For example, they might say, "I like eat" instead of "I would like to eat." Those who spoke standard English called the mixed speech "pidgin."

At about twelve years of age, children were given tests to find out how well they spoke English. Those who passed the test were sent to schools called English Standard. These were much better than ordinary schools. They had the finest buildings and playgrounds and libraries. The best teachers taught in them.

The English Standard test was easy for most white students to pass. They were born into families that had always spoken English so they learned from birth to speak it correctly. But the test was terribly hard for Asians. Only a few passed it.

Whites were able to make this unfair system work because they had money and power. They held important jobs as bankers and judges and newspaper publishers. They owned most of the big plantations and factories and the huge shipping companies. They ran the territorial legislature.

The English Standard test played a large part in keeping Asians poor and powerless in Hawaii. The test made it very hard for their children to get as good an education as most white children. And without that Asian children had little chance of getting better jobs and living better lives than their parents when they grew up.

Yet Dan Inouye dared to hope. Even though he was not admitted to an English Standard school, he intended to become a doctor. He admired as heroes two doctors who had been important in his life. Dr. Sato, a Japanese, had cared gently for Dan's grandmother when she was sick. Dr. Craig, a white, refused money for a difficult operation he did on Dan's arm when it was broken.

Dan wanted to become a surgeon and perform operations to help people. It was a high ambition for a nisei boy from a poor family, but Dan was determined. He wanted to do something useful and important with his life. He read all the books he could find on doctors and medicine.

He took a first aid course to learn how to care for people who were sick or hurt.

But when Dan was seventeen years old, something happened that changed everything.

On December 7, 1941, Japanese planes bombed the United States navy base at Pearl Harbor in Hawaii.

It happened early on a Sunday morning. Dan heard the news on the radio. At first he could not believe that something so terrible could happen. But when he ran outside he knew that it was true. He could hear the dull thuds of bombs exploding, and the *ack-ack* of anti-aircraft guns. Huge clouds of smoke puffed over Pearl Harbor.

Dan watched in horror as planes rose out of the smoke to fly away from the damage they had done. As they streaked through the blue sky in neat formations, Dan saw red balls painted on their wings. He knew they stood for the rising sun of the Japanese empire.

The bombing sank or damaged most of the ships in Pearl Harbor. It killed more than two thousand people. And it plunged the United States into World War II, a war that had already begun in Europe.

The Japanese attack was a terrible shock and a great tragedy for all Americans. But it was especially painful for Americans of Japanese descent. They felt shame and

anger at what the country of their ancestors had done. They knew, too, that many whites would not trust them to be loyal to the United States. Some people would suspect them of wanting Japan to win the war because they were of Japanese descent. Some would be cruel enough to call them "dirty Japs."

Like most young Japanese-American men, Dan's first thought was to prove his loyalty by joining the United States army. But for over a year he was not allowed to enlist. Nisei were not trusted to serve in the armed forces.

Dan got a job as a medical aide because he had taken first aid. He worked from six in the evening to six in the morning. He went to school during the day and slept when he could. He did not mind being tired. It was much worse to feel that he was not trusted.

Then suddenly the rule was changed. The news came that nisei would now be accepted into the army. Four thousand nisei from Hawaii and the U.S. mainland would form a combat team to fight in the front lines.

Dan rushed to sign up. When his orders came, he was sent on a ship across the Pacific Ocean to Mississippi. There he trained to become a soldier. The training was tough but the young nisei wanted it that way. They felt that it was not enough for them to be good soldiers. They

thought that they had to prove their loyalty by being the very best.

Thirteen months later Dan boarded a troop ship to cross the Atlantic Ocean to Italy. There he would fight Germans and Italians who were on the side of Japan in the war.

Dan's unit was the 442nd Combat Team, better known as the "Go for Broke" battalion. The nickname was their slogan, which means to give it all you've got. And the young men did just that. The 442nd became famous as

one of the bravest units of the United States army. It was made up entirely of nisei.

Dan was such a good soldier that he was made an officer. But he never got used to men killing other men. For him, fighting was a hateful job that had to be done.

The enemy was driven back, but the war went on and on. Dan led his men in hard and dangerous fighting. They slogged through mud and they slept in ditches. Day after day they fought the Germans, hill by hill, from village to village.

In April 1945, eleven days before the enemy surrendered in Europe, Dan led his men up a ridge held by Germans. A bullet smashed into his right elbow. It almost tore his arm off. Yet Dan kept fighting, using his left hand to fire his gun. He did not stop until he was sure that his men could take and keep the hill.

Dan won the Distinguished Service Cross medal for his bravery, but doctors could not save his arm. It had to be cut off. With it went Dan's dream of becoming a surgeon. A doctor needs two hands to operate.

Dan spent many months in hospitals learning to live with one arm. He learned to write left-handed, to tie his shoelaces, and to use a knife and fork. He learned to play the piano with one hand, and to drive a car.

In army hospitals Dan came to know haoles as friends for the first time. He found it did not matter that their skin was white. They laughed at the same jokes he did. They had the same fears and worries.

Dan's haole friends liked and admired the one-armed nisei captain who never felt sorry for himself. They decided to teach him some things they thought he ought to know. They loaned him books they felt he should read. They kidded him about talking pidgin until he was willing to let them help him improve his English. He practiced until he sounded as though he had spoken English all his life.

Now that Dan could not become a surgeon, he had to decide what he would do instead. He made up his mind to go to law school. He felt that the study of law would best prepare him for what he now hoped would be his future. He wanted to go into politics. New laws would be needed in a world changed by the war. Dan wanted to help make those laws.

He joined the Democratic party. He believed it to be the political party that would help Asians gain rights to the same education and jobs as other Americans. The Democratic party had never been strong in Hawaii. Republicans had always controlled the territorial legislature. But now more and more Asians were signing up to vote, and they were declaring themselves Democrats.

There was new hope, too, that Congress might at last take Hawaii into the union as a state. Those against statehood claimed that Hawaii was not truly American because

half its people were Asians with loyalties to other countries. But the war had made it clear that this argument was untrue. Asians had proved themselves good and patriotic citizens.

Most people in Hawaii were eager for statehood. They believed they had earned the right to govern themselves and to send representatives to Washington who could vote in Congress. Everyone felt sure that statehood would come someday. But when?

After twenty months in hospitals, Dan was able to go home. Now he could get on with his education. He became a student at the University of Hawaii.

In the winter of 1947 Dan fell in love with a pretty Japanese-American teacher named Margaret Awamura. Dan and Maggie were married at the end of Dan's third year of college.

A year later they sailed on a ship to the United States. Dan was going to law school at George Washington University. He chose it because it was in Washington, D.C. The nation's capital was the best place to learn about politics.

Dan often went to Capitol Hill to watch Congress at work. As he sat in the balcony of the Senate or the House of Representatives, he learned how laws are made.

After Dan graduated from law school, he and Maggie returned to Hawaii where Dan got his first job as a lawyer.

An election was coming up in 1954. There was a feeling in the air that it was going to be a different sort of election. It looked as though Democrats had a chance to win more seats than ever before in the territorial legislature. Dan wanted to help. He went to Democratic meetings to talk about ideas and plans.

One night it was suggested that Dan run for a seat in the territorial House of Representatives. This surprised him. He planned to run for office someday, but not so soon. He was not well known. He was not yet thirty years old.

"Why me?" he asked. "There are lots of others better known."

"Because you can win," his supporters told him. "War veterans will vote for you because you're one of them. They know you'll work for the things they fought for."

Dan knew that it would not be an easy race. In the fifty-six years since Hawaii became a territory, his district had elected only two Democrats. But he agreed to try. "I'll give it all I've got," he said.

It was the old "Go for Broke" spirit, and the other candidates had it, too. They worked hard and made many speeches. They talked about statehood. They said that there must be no more second-class citizens living in slums and working for low pay. Dan spoke quietly but people listened to him. They felt that he meant what he said.

On election night the long years of Republican rule came to an end. Democrats won most of the seats in both the territorial House of Representatives and the Senate. Dan Inouye got the most votes of all.

He served in the territorial House in Hawaii for four years. In 1958 he ran for a seat in the Senate and won again.

At last, in 1959, the United States Congress passed a bill granting statehood to Hawaii. A new star was added to the flag as Hawaii became the fiftieth state. Bells rang, horns tooted, and people cheered throughout Hawaii as the new flag with fifty stars was raised.

Now Hawaii could elect two senators and a representative to the Congress in Washington, D.C. Each state, big or small, elects two United States senators. But the number of representatives it elects depends on the number of people who live in the state. New York elects thirty-nine. In 1959, Hawaii elected only one.

Daniel Inouye became the first Congressman from the state of Hawaii.

On his first day in the House of Representatives, he walked down the aisle to face the Speaker, whose desk was on a raised platform at the front of the big room. He was to take the oath of office.

The Speaker said, as he always did at a swearing-in ceremony, "Raise your right hand and repeat after me."

But Daniel Inouye could not do that. It was his left hand he raised as he repeated the words, "I, Daniel Ken Inouye, do solemnly swear that I will support and defend the Constitution of the United States."

Much of the work in Congress is done by committees. The Foreign Affairs Committee is considered one of the most powerful. But Congressman Inouye turned down a chance to be on it. He asked, instead, to be appointed to the Committee on Agriculture. This surprised people, but to Hawaii with its huge sugar and pineapple industries, agriculture is all-important. Daniel Inouye cared more about serving the people of his state than he did about gaining power for himself.

In 1962 he was elected to the Senate for a six-year term. In the Senate he has worked tirelessly for civil rights laws and for better understanding among nations. He feels that population control is one of the most important keys to world peace.

To make his point, he tells a story about the squirrels

who live in the woods outside his house. One day he noticed the squirrels fighting over the food he set out for them. He began giving them more food and the fighting stopped. The squirrels, the Senator said, were not so different from humans. People, too, need enough for everyone to have a rightful share. Unless we keep down the number of people in the world, there will not be enough food to go around. Then countries without enough land to grow the crops they need will go to war to take land away from other countries.

Senator Inouye served as a member of the Senate Watergate Committee. It was formed to find out if crimes had been committed during President Nixon's 1972 election campaign. The Watergate hearings were on television, and Senator Inouye's deep voice and quick smile became known to viewers all over the world. He was always calm and dignified and well prepared. The Watergate hearings led to Richard Nixon's resignation as President.

The people of Hawaii like and approve of their hardworking Senator. At election time, they vote in huge numbers to send him back for another term in the Senate.

To Senator Inouye one of the most important events of his life was the birth in 1964 of his son, Daniel Ken Inouye, Junior. The Senator wrote a book for Ken which he called *Journey to Washington*. It is the story of his life.

He wrote it because he wanted Ken to know the boy his father once was, and to understand how he became the man he is today.

The Senator still raises tropical fish as he did when he was a boy in Hawaii. He has seven tanks of them in his house in Maryland near Washington, D.C. It is a nice house with a garden planted with many flowering trees.

As a United States Senator, Daniel Inouye is an important man. He is welcome anywhere he chooses to go. But he has not forgotten what it was like to grow up a Japanese-American in the slums of Hawaii. In the Senate of the United States, he works for laws that assure equal rights to all people of all races.

ABOUT THE AUTHOR

Jane Goodsell, the author of DANIEL INOUYE, was born in Portland, Oregon, and has lived most of her life there. She has written books and many magazine articles for both children and adults and presently writes a syndicated weekly humorous column. She is the mother of three daughters.

"I became an admirer of Senator Inouye during the Watergate hearings," Mrs. Goodsell notes, "became even more of an admirer when I read his book, *Journey to Washington*, and liked him enormously when I met him and had a chance to talk to him."

ABOUT THE ILLUSTRATOR

Haru Wells was born in Buenos Aires, Argentina. She studied painting, sculpture, and drawing there, and later taught art and worked independently in design, puppetry, and sculpture. After a year of study at the Hornsey College of Art in London, she came to New York City, where she lived until her recent move to Dallas, Texas. Ms. Wells has produced and directed animated cartoons for "Sesame Street," and now is a free-lance illustrator specializing in children's books, audiovisual material, and design.

NOTE TO PARENTS

Learning to read is an important skill for all children. It is a big milestone that you can help your child reach. The Richard Scarry Easy Reader program is designed to support you and your child through this process. Developed by reading specialists, each book in the series includes carefully selected words and sentence structures to help children advance from beginner to intermediate to proficient readers.

Here are some tips to keep in mind as you read these books with your child:

First, preview the book together. Read the title. Then look at the cover. Ask your child, "What is happening on the cover? What do you think this book is about?"

Next, skim through the pages of the book and look at the illustrations. This will help your child use the illustrations to understand the story.

Then encourage your child to read. If he or she stumbles over words, try some of these strategies:

- **Use the pictures as clues**
- **Point out words that are repeated**
- **Sound out difficult words**
- **Break up bigger words into smaller chunks**
- **Use the context to lend meaning**

Finally, find out if your child understands what he or she is reading. After you have finished reading, ask, "What happened in this book?"

Above all, understand that each child learns to read at a different rate. Make sure to praise your young reader and provide encouragement along the way!

LEVEL 1

Introduce Your Child to Reading
Simple words and simple sentences encourage beginning readers to sound out words.

LEVEL 2

Your Child Starts to Read
Slightly more difficult words in simple sentences help new readers build confidence.

LEVEL 3

Your Child Reads with Help
More complex words and sentences and longer text lengths help young readers reach reading proficiency.

RICHARD SCARRY'S
Great Big Schoolhouse
Readers

Hop, Hop, and Away!

Illustrated by Huck Scarry
Written by Erica Farber

STERLING CHILDREN'S BOOKS
New York

Today is show-and-tell.

Huckle packed his backpack.

2

Huckle packed his lunch.

Huckle packed his pet frog.

Hop, hop, and away!

Huckle's frog hopped away.

Lowly got the frog.

Phew!

Good job, Lowly!

Huckle went to school.

Hop, hop, and away!

Huckle's frog hopped away.

Skip got the frog.

Thank you, Skip!

It was time for show-and-tell.

Show & Tell

Arthur showed
his ant farm.

Ella showed her fancy doll.

Bridget had a whistle.

Bridget blew it.

10

Hop, hop, and away!

Huckle's frog hopped away.

It hopped on Ella. Oh, no!

Huckle got his frog.

It was not his turn.

Lowly was next.

He told a joke.

Molly showed a book.

Skip had a big ball.

He bounced the ball.

Bam! Bam!

Frances had a volcano.

She put stuff into it.

At last it was Huckle's turn.

He showed his frog.

BOOM! went the volcano.

BOOM! BOOM!

Lava went up in the air.

Lava went all over.

Bridget blew
her whistle.

Hop, hop, and away!

Huckle's frog hopped away.

It hopped on Skip.

Bam went Skip's ball.

The ball hit Molly's book.

The book hit the ant farm.

BOOM! CRASH!

Hop, hop, and away!
Huckle's frog hopped
on Miss Honey.

She smiled.

Then it was time to clean up.

This was the best show-and-tell ever!

STERLING CHILDREN'S BOOKS
New York

An Imprint of Sterling Publishing
387 Park Avenue South
New York, NY 10016

ISBN 978-1-4549-1310-8

Produced by

 JR Sansevere

Distributed in Canada by Sterling Publishing
C/o Canadian Manda Group, 165 Dufferin Street
Toronto, Ontario, Canada M6K 3H6
Distributed in the United Kingdom by GMC Distribution Services
Castle Place, 166 High Street, Lewes, East Sussex, England BN7 1XU
Distributed in Australia by Capricorn Link (Australia) Pty. Ltd.
P.O. Box 704, Windsor, NSW 2756, Australia

For information about custom editions, special sales, premium and corporate purchases,
please contact Sterling Special Sales at 800-805-5489 or specialsales@sterlingpublishing.com.

Printed in China

Lot #:
2 4 6 8 10 9 7 5 3 1
12/13

www.sterlingpublishing.com/kids

24

RICHARD SCARRY'S
Great Big Schoolhouse
Readers

One of the best-selling children's author/illustrators of all time, Richard Scarry has taught generations of children about the world around them—from the alphabet to counting, identifying colors, and even exploring a day at school.

Though Scarry's books are educational, they are beloved for their charming characters, wacky sense of humor, and frenetic energy. Scarry considered himself an entertainer first, and an educator second. He once said, "Everything has an educational value if you look for it. But it's the FUN I want to get across."

A prolific artist, Richard Scarry created more than 300 books, and they have sold over 200 million copies worldwide and have been translated into 30 languages. Richard Scarry died in 1994, but his incredible legacy continues with new books illustrated by his son, Huck Scarry.